NOTES FROM TOYOTA-LAND